Hush Sessions

Kristi Maxwell

saturnalia books

Saturnalia Books
105 Woodside Rd.
Ardmore, PA 19003
info@saturnaliabooks.com

ISBN: 978-0-9818591-3-2
Library of Congress Control Number: 2009930091

Book Design by Saturnalia Books
Printing by Westcan Printing Group, Canada

Cover Art by Elisabeth Timpone.

Distributed by:
University Press of New England
1 Court Street
Lebanon, NH 03766
800-421-1561

Grateful acknowledgement is made to the editors of the following journals, in which poems from this manuscript (some in earlier versions) first appeared:

42opus : *"Braid"*
The Concher : *excerpt from "Hush Sessions"*
Backwards City Review : *excerpt from "Hush Sessions"*
Madison Review : *"Dominant"*
La Fovea : excerpt from *"Hush Sessions"*
No Tell Motel : *"Sarcophagus"* (*:To the bed, :Always, :Night hawks);"Seasoned"*
Spinning Jenny : *"Like the Earth, 2/3rds Water;"* "Imperative" (published as part of "Like the Earth, 2/3rds Water")
Spork : *"Log of Dead Birds",* "Survey" (published as part of *"Log of Dead Birds"*)

"Dominant" was awarded Madison Review's 2005 Phyllis Smart Young Prize.

"Sarcophagus : To the bed" also appears in the anthology *The Bedside Guide to No Tell Motel –
2nd Floor* (eds. Reb Livingston and Molly Arden, No Tell Books, 2007).

The excerpt from "Hush Sessions" first printed in *Backwards City Review* was reprinted on *Verse Daily*.

My gratitude to all of those who helped this book to be and who supported me during its writing and many revisions. For their insight and time, special thanks to Michael Rerick, Marty Hebrank, TC Tolbert, Theresa Sotto, Dawn Pendergast, Barbara Cully, Ann Fine, and Ashley VanDoorn. My gratitude also to Henry Israeli and everyone at Saturnalia Books.

for my mother & my father

Table of Contents

≈

"Superstition is to believe what you see to believe what
you hear and to see what you see.
    That makes superstition clear.
    And in a way yes in a way it has nothing to do with human nature
or the human mind.
    Superstition exists in itself because it is so true."

—Gertrude Stein, *The Geographical History of America*

The impulse

to forecast as with weather

whether the debris of birds not breathing matters

as concerns one's matter: conference of cells gelled in being

who is: a flu that symptoms — who?

who is: the forehead that heaves the heat away?

log of dead birds

A wing as a bird.

A wing that catches the wind like the end of a conversation

and responds this way.

When I say bring your arm to bed

the invitation's extended to the not-arm of you.

My body is less polite.

A wing as a mouth you con me with.

I enact a minnow-shaped cabin you press into.

We plane.

Whose resistance feigns air flight demands?

Two of my birds are not real
as in birds that have been.
I say dead, for evaluation's sake.

One entry: hallelujah, like mallard, or robin.

Feathers do not shard and aren't avoided as glass as wheels
wheel from the parking lot.

Roadwork revises our arrival.
A detour through a small Texas town.

The mixed tape made for Xmas
vacations through its ribbon then returns to
Tom Waits, and the diner again,
us—pondering the ransacked nest
balanced in my uterus.

This birdlessness.

I apologize if Xmas offends you.
I would have written out Christmas
but it is Xmas in my log because
very little space between margins—
these are not childbearing margins.

Winter obscures birds for obvious reasons. I've compromised
my location haven't I. In a clinic

tv placement determines migration. (...winter scours
the chimney) A talk show

skips so you know it's recorded. (...with wings we hear
scratch) The talk show repeats: When Faith Saved Your Life.

It's meant to be a kindness from the staff (...until we hear
the wings not scratch)—easier to draw blood if

the patient's relaxed as a word
cradled in the nook of an apostrophe, its recliner shape so cozy.

The claim isn't I see more, but I notice
more of my seeing — *i* is my needle inside bird —
I draw meaning.

This vial act tires me.
So I'll listen.

Windchimes wrapped in tissue illustrate:
it's not no sound, but the not hearing of sound.

I see your point.

My sympathy's with fabric during the hem:
point-sick, and pinned.

Listen — this bird thing is no joke.

But I'll ease you in with bird jokes, made up in bed:

A bird stores sugar? In a toucan-ister.
A bird strolls into a dollar store and cheeps: Cheep!

I make of a mouth how a face interprets longitude
and fillets these human-feigning countries with mood.
Happiness, Sadness — which north, which south?

Laughter strips my face and carts the cargo of teeth to the open deck.

Do an inventory check if you want, but I'll just tell you:
twenty-eight. I slide my tongue over them
when I get nervous.

See, I'm sliding my tongue.

If you think this is a puzzle, you're mistaken.

I intended to make a table so you'd trust me—
to strand all my information on the table like a firearm,
my hands in view.

It would have looked like this:

event	sample	conclusion
[an occurrence]	[details to represent the occurrence]	[the significance the occurrence has gained through evaluation]

The beak-poised hand.

The *were* of birds field-sketched
into words.

I feel most confident about my pigeon-on-its-back assessment.

Within two days of the sighting, there's a phone call
from a man, and the man is frantic.

The man is not always the same, but the man is always frantic.

Neither is the man always frantic about the same thing.

Most recently: *you need to—*, so do.
Needle need. Blood needed, for telling.

And so a number. To be numbered among
other numbers, then called. Culled.

Number Eight a few scats away
in keeping with real numbers.

She eyes me like a red light
before wading out to make a right turn.

If Number were surname
I might understand
her insistence
to connect.

excuse me, it's just, you look like such a nice…

as if niceness is an exemption.
The laugh track played to mask the fact
an audience doesn't react.
A statistics book asserts fifty
the minimum sample size
for accurate hypotheses

though conviction convinces with one eyewitness.

The raven skull was a rarity I spared in a Ziploc bag.

On rocks and from a distance, a raven skull and a hamburger wrapper
are not so different.

Oregon Coast, near Devil's Elbow
near Devil's Compass and Spine.

Superstitions insist *raven* synonymous with *ominous*
but death recasts a body as bone.
The bird decomposes into salutation: *ave* (Latin).

The way light's watered down to something to read by.

An eyelid's the original lampshade, lowered to create mood.
Sad is this much eye.

My eye aces this game: an iris noses the corner and you know I'm guilty.

A metal handrail adjusts snow to after-a-slight-rain—

why aren't you a metal handrail, or better yet
why aren't mistakes warmed to the swipe.

You can't not see a dead bird after you have seen it:
that defies the laws of eye.

Pigeon-Not-On-Its-Back is how I knew I'd lose you.

There are various ways to remember things.
Photograph is specific within the various.

We laid on our backs with the lens focused on a high window
where enough shade created the story of a body,
of a hand reaching for an asterisk of snow.

An asterisk between us:

the symbol used to mark a structure believed to have existed, but un-
recorded, or recorded incorrectly.

A phonebook exacerbates fate:

you are just one proton floating in the element of your name.
If the number tried first is the right one—.

A safe's combination is superfluous with cash on the counter.

Someone waits for your carelessness like a walk signal.

If you think Pigeon-Not-On-Its-Back = loss
you're missing something.

Loss is not consistently good
or consistently bad:

I lost my car keys [situation: hurry]

She lost fifteen pounds [situation: a doctor's recommendation]

He lost a tooth [situation: tooth fairy]

He lost a tooth [situation: fist]

It equals loss + this-much-eye [the sad-width, remember].

You tell me mayonnaise is the only reliable thing
and I want to be oily and white and in
your mouth.

The house was made of wood so the Christmas tree seemed
funny as

pinheads of sand glammed up behind glass,
framed there.

Perhaps alerts tradition out of its starting position and around the track.

See, the angel does look more luminous
when branches are bare.

Bearing down differentiates a branch from a twig—the mouth that bears,
the size of the mouth.

Desire deals with wingspan—
that it has a bigger or smaller, but which is it,
I always get this wrong

it matters for binocular adjustment.

The first time I saw the Grand Canyon was Thanksgiving.

A day after seeing a bird
I refer to by color and size
because I can't figure its name.

Size: rice bowl (the one with fish etchings where earrings are kept)

I've concluded Red-Chested/Rice Bowl a holiday bird.

I'll save you some trouble: if in, or purposed toward, the oven
turkeys are not in the log.

Otherwise the grocery store deli would be too easy to manipulate.

Buses and RVs that go through the Grand Canyon's guardrails
and can't be removed are spray-painted
to safeguard the view.

A bald eagle nest nine feet across and twenty-seven feet deep.

You hold—no I cannot fathom your hold.

The last time we agreed it never happened.
Maintenance is a lack of specifics (and lack, specific).
A specific like like. Like *buttonquail.*

The pygmy owl from the toy bin
at the museum I named heartache and balanced

on the lamp
so I could say

heartache looks over my bed.
Faith is frozen

goldfish in a bowl thawed
on the Formica counter.

Give it fifteen minutes.
Fins cat-door, and swim paws in.

I learn you like a floodlight a certain distance avoids
setting off:

how you shiver like teeth or a wire
made electric by the exit of birds.

To be the cold that holds you
like teeth—

by roots or ruse.

Survey

When I called it a log, did you see it barked with flapping?

And this?: <O
        OXX=
       _/]

≈

Sarcophagus

: To the bed

amounts to porchlight. The sidewalk
muddled through his hair. Our weapon is these: my this
on his, his this on this like a marriage not stretched out as Ten-
nessee
but more

the notch Ohio is. Near
a pond superfluous
with cod. These. Nearer me, he never mouths open

at morning. For the breath
secure as a bench
my tongue could sit on but for the wet.
Yes, the rains are again. The bed

is mounted by porchlight. So I can't sleep
says translucent eyelids, like awkward fish
where the ocean drained. To his I do

I do the bed like a sheet. That the cord can dictate light
we don't complain about. What long fingers
margin his touch,
dedicated as this bulb
to fishing

my waking. He sleeps through
and through, like a good kind
of genuine—that is not proof
the gold is

: Night hawks

its eye-time. What he looks like
because his computer commutes
my seeing. This is a fun time! I tell him
when the wind makeshifts a skirt around me
while a hawk adorns its talons
with mouse and crushes our simple idea of bulbs
devious with their dangling light. He looks least.
Our cat befriends cement — its fur furthers the distance
to flesh. That he is unlined as an autumn
jacket! Such might
I wear.

: *Always*

somebody's too-red meat
beats me for most tender
as he earnestly to himself says
"tend to her" and affixes his hand
on skin I clear my clothes from
the way twigs around a pit
that become tinder for it

: *O flashing light*

nigh against the flesh-taut sky
or what a knee might
to an x-ray
do. These within-stars
wintering where eyes can't go
without a white screen
backlit. And something lifted
there.

≈

Like the Earth, 2/3rds Water

Fertile: soil imposed on the body more pond-ish than dock

In fertile: yes, get in:

a hangar where the cargo plane shuttles

but the egg: wingless and without pilot

empty is the inevitable the hangar was built for

what is this urge to break open
and feel what you know is there:

he felt my long-stemmed rib as if
to gather a bone bouquet,

my fingers clavicle-plunged
but it was useless as a fish trying to poke its nose
through an ice-callused pond.

when a mountain shakes out its slopes, say *valley*
when the bed is finally made, say *sleep is a fax machine for dreams*
when the body apologizes: *soap-stained silverware*

Aortic Valve—   yes, I resort to your full name

the heart is not   a giving machine

such primitive conveyer belts: veins

what body's not   a mass production

I'd like to see the supervisor   systems do seem the best system

for instance: government   as if branches sprout the trunk

executive   judicial   legislative   the body has nine

which should have clued me into "no"   sounds like   *nein*

sounds like   blood, where are you?

in Siena a plaza's divided for clan identification   seventeen folds that make the fan

a body's fluids are less   fraternal

blame your orifices,   those offices malled along your strip,

and their revolving doors   that attend more to exit than entrance

each orifice demands samples   like wallpaper swatches, or carpet

the fairest divvy is straws   my ovaries attempted   paper rock

scissors   but could only manage rock

so neither wins   a thing

sleep   where tomorrow is boarded   when you wake, you wake

an inch taller   each vertebrae is

by airline policy   allowed two pieces of carry-on luggage

if that helps you   sense the extra inch   to some extent I'm kidding

which is kidding too   I can't   kid   thus the addition interest

rational: understandable in terms that accord with logic or scientific knowledge

ration: the divvy   to which you are privy

mouth, its saliva share   eye-ducts like birthday cards stuffed with money

pores trough across skin, each with its personal salt block   sweat-feed

stupid he said, cunt with its three shares   not even nostrils are so bold

a bladder detour   slower traffic keep right   he goes to the bathroom

before he goes to me   necessity cracks its whip—   you're a good rider

is the horse real is not relevant   the plural of my body is no:

July: no   August: no   September   through August: more no than fingers

a mutant little hand of no   on the hook,

no scrim of worm   my blood absent, and without a doctor's excuse

blood   a ball stuck in a pool table   a room crammed with knobs misses doors

anesthesia sounds the room like a video game   points accumulate

a whole microscope plate of points   look—how warmly the syringe surrogates blood:

there you are,   hello

If a name is inaccurate it is ornamental:

indulge me the dictionary as it charades my name

first syllable—max: the maximum limit or amount of something

second syllable—well (n.): a source of a freely and abundantly available supply of something, a container, a compartment that is used to store something temporarily

well (v.): to surge from within so as to threaten to burst forth

well (adv.): indicating something is performed in a satisfactory way

well (adj.): mentally and physically healthy

we'll (contraction): we [a pronoun that refers to at least two people] will

name versus a diagnosis [no wedged even there]

a ghost presses its fingers against a mirror and surprise, no prints—mess depends on mass

In its shell, the egg cannot be eaten.
No one said pick up a carton of yolks.

most say I have my mother's body I am
denied it three times
there's a rooster inside me—
crow, baby, crow

Imperative

antibodies oust the virus from a body—

pro-body antibodies

I virus I
vie

to keep you

Olly-olly-oxen-free : when I asked your body to parrot
this is the phrase I had in mind.

I thought sometimes we'd substitute *artery* for *oxen-free*
so the route embeds the plea.

Today we played *veins* with the sidewalks: our sweaters
dictate the roles—

you were in white, so leukocyte. I clotted your mouth.

Continuance—yes I begrudge certain functions their tools,
that the voice gets a container

       and my fingers aren't libraries where *feel* can be archived.
Sequel's allegiance is with bad movies.

That is to say: if I could part-two you, disease wouldn't flock
to your big screen.

In the flames: hands, always hands.
It throws them across the wall—

I'm convinced my fingers are
the creatures they construct.

My eyes,
sockets clogged with eye,

with you—standing
like water

still.

Hush Sessions

Hold the light up to me like something small, she said.
Rinds were slippery beneath his fingers and his fingernails
slipped in. His concern was the white tent tooth-like at the back
of the farm his arm could obliterate if lifted near
to his eyes as the smallness she wanted. The telescope was his favorite form
of aggression, or the bag game. How she reached in and the air
didn't feel remarkable, despite his insistence she mark
her findings with the little pen which of them uncapped.

The day of the experiment, they had not bathed.
He brought the equation out and sat it like birthday cake
onto the bench. Then the preparing of the anthem the way knobs
to the right heat. They sang it over lunch: loose packets of amen—
a fuse not to be refused, a fuse not to be...& so on.
It wasn't a very good hymn—nonetheless they ducked on high
notes, like something were going off
above them. Debris flaked off their tongues.

He stole boxes off their packed things. Her disapproval
didn't take. In a bonfire that looked like a glass
when he stood over it and looked down
is where he stashed them. It was his third sculpture
called The Detriment of Ice. The forecast of rain
pained her for that. He renamed it

Our Hyphen Jealousies

in scorn of their gloves.
She did not approve for different reasons,
though of different reasons
she was fine with.

A thermos boasted its contents—and she liked that enough
to mimic with her blouse. He called his thirst
into question. He pulled the comfy bed from the comfortable couch
his reclining broke the hierarchy between. If they had a pool
they agreed to understand one another underwater for a length of time
measured by what sun can do to skin

instead of the other option. She brought a bird home
that handed its beak over like an ingredient. They passed
the bird between them and read passages that sounded like wings
in turn.

The moon was nothing to feel sorry for, she was sure.
She took a table from the alley without its accompanying chairs.
All he asked was the window be described by the yard.

Stop collecting the grass like postcards, he would say
to the most fertile mounds of dirt. Propellers,
she corrected him, propellers, and prepared her arms.
They brought their voices to the volume of bread—blade-shaped
and sawing, sawing.

On the carpet she sat in a way that suggested carpet, and he
near her knee. She detected him the way joints
allowed. If he were a storm, then she

a field shot-up with poppies.

Heave, her mouth punched out, and he did. She slashed it with pleasure
into the doorframe where a height might go. Her heave bartered
with his coaxing. They named this entry What Air Can Do
To Sacks, or To Be Perceived As Empty. The year shifted like a clause.
Such countdowns they fashioned
through their lungs!

She agreed she would only be she three days of the week.
He agreed he would be only he as many. On Tuesdays
he called her limb, which she liked like the wet center
of a poached egg, which she liked.

The fireplace was just a place these days
that embers felt secure in, whose favorite was this,
during the argument that distracted them as they waited
for wind to take the umbrella they waited
to miss.

Cold. Cold. Cold. It went back and forth like this until
nothing. She considered what standing resembles
a flamingo. She tried a new approach: shrimp, three times aloud

allowed out to air, and the shivering began, then the color
attributed to a brain, but in places for touching.

He waded through her little sea of calluses. Understand
she could not feel him. The doctor was called in
who admired the way eyelashes gathered with cat hair
on the felt. We own a cat, they said. Ah, so this is not
the problem, surmised this hired him who admired her liver
still as a steak. He laid his stethoscope naughtily
against her chest, and to her dismay, geese laid
their tiny flesh-eggs on her.

He got that a rocket was meant to love the ground
as a shirt would, if thrown there. He assured her
and she wept. He assured her
she should not weep
for this, but her eyes were caught
like an arm in this big machine of tears. Is this not beautiful,
she asked, as she refused a napkin.
His handkerchief was nearby, which he did not hand her.
The trees were too petty to blossom
when weeping latched onto him—she passed
a plate for what might form petals in their falling.

The house decorated like a teacup no longer
spilled into particular rooms. He was tired she was tired.

Then the combs began—there was something secretive
about them, something rocklike toward her window-dark hair.
Plastic teeth scripted oaths over her own. Ambassadors,
she said, her hair at rest, then, to him,
the bicycles have become useless fountains.

Buckets weighted down her hands.

It was a very over the shoulder way of dealing with it,
but the wine key came out anyway
like something esteemed. Who shall, you shall
was the shallow hollering they committed
under the awning, until one of them froze.
He admitted her imitation of a baseball mitt
very convincing. Until what jutted toward her.

All the lights come on as headaches—the bulbs must go,
who said, whose demands dismantled such. There were many
of these brief vacations through the cupboard. They enjoyed
the way things felt in their hands.

The blue tablecloth was a gift. He had taken to globes.
They took turns over a glass stuffed with olives over
the tablecloth. June has the best shape to it, she insisted.
He made a calculator with each button
a version of June. Numbers were none.

They were careful as prepositions with each other
when the gifts grew dull. In an innocent manner one inquired
of the corridor, lengthwise, a throat could become.
Whoever finds a ghost for it first

was their bet.

Stave

Nietzsche insists *sickness can be
a stimulant*—that feeling one gets when in
a snake-mimicked bridge (*simulacrum*, rattle crumb
-les, rathers itself as feet, as those flickering).

Vertigo, flesh pinwheel, gearshift.
Eavesdropping throws listening into reverse—

your name and this-long-left,
brake-slammed heart.

If ear sounds like hear,
are the other senses
insensible?
The mouth can't be trusted
because it says—

it doesn't matter.
There's a word-map on my tongue:
U.S.S.R.—that's an old map,
where something existed.

We stuff ourselves into
agreement—

don't die I won't die well if you don't well of course one of us

a tat death picks at until the whole thing's ruined,
one long string and no knitting hooks.

Repair (genetic): The Great Wall
an architectural stem cell—

One-tenth its original size. Stones broken off
for new.

Side roads develop from the alphabet—
we develop
short cuts to avoid sentences

involving time,
involving medical terms with uncertain
pronunciations.

A name's given to yell
across the sidewalk—you is careless—
I call the male dog an it out of spite.

The goal of a leash
is to achieve the same result
without it. The good boy.
A face that doesn't flinch
at a hand —illness muzzles
your body and you let it tug

tug tug
you around.
Your heart divided into four squares

blood bounces between (one to one to one to one)—what's bound

to go out of?
I am asking—
don't take off, ignore the intercom

your name, your name and please come— : La La La La (my hands over your ears)

≈

Braid

on chronology's wrist
               sits this gaudy minute
        fiddled like a clasp—
                   it's the soap again
slipping out the window
               pigeon-holed an antonym
        of clean; what do you
                   cling to the way the wet
clotheslines hope for; such
               soft perches scoped out
        on another body;
                   a towel white enough
to blizzard; what turns
               a massacre into a mass acre sulking
        with silt; shag carpet remedies
                   easily what needs obscured –
knees purge standing
               and thin to kneel:
        forgive the greed I build
               in my mouth
—you're coming on permanent,
               like strong; whose hair wrote

the history of combs

documented behind

a plus parading

as a crucifix stud, pinned

—a private altar

skin inherits

dominant

A collector hones in on the kink in production:
text printed backward, a doll's hand
attached in place of a foot.
Multiple copies of the (seemingly) same thing,
names no longer matter.

He's a husband made up of wife molecules—
molecular ceremony:
(n.): a group of [humans] [legally] bonded together, representing the [most
restricted] fundamental unit of a compound that can take part in an
[amorous] reaction

—who collects things aside from wives (though seven accumulate).
Businesses: jewelry, antiques, farm,
pawnshop:

> jade glassware, thimbles, service pumps from old gas stations,
> a Playboy with Marilyn Monroe. And marbles—his expertise—
> the way he learned to touch a line without crossing it—stringing
> of affection like a tightrope—even one misplaced step, and—

Over here, the display case of wives:

> The First: her boy-fetus removed like excessive digits
> of a rounded-off number.
> The Second: chain-link of x chromosomes. Girl girl girl.
> (Marriage-as-interview: hired, fired, hired again. Position filled
> before available. The affairs begin like links added
> in a watchband though it's already loose.)
> The Third: _____.

Work through it like a math problem:

> If his letter to the Second reads god intended for us three to be
> together, all I ask is you honor his decision, and she answers yes,
> then the babysitter moves in. If the women are to become friends,
> they vacation without him. A ski-lift spines up the slumped landscape.
> Sea foam curves like a backbone along the shore. (In this way,
> the equation is not spineless.) Now, who would place the call home to him?
> (*I-love-you* thrown like a hot potato.) Now, if his daughters also play?

Because numbers are taken, a key for his children:

> X, first
> Y, second
> Z, third

Q: Describe your father.
> X : I moved my room to the second floor to get away from Elvis' face
> pressed against my window. It seems important you know
> I never thought my dad was Elvis. That wasn't singing.

Y : A dance floor empty on slow songs. Fear a corsage
> that punctures a breast during the pin.

Q: And when his mistress lived with you?
> X : Mother had this shirt—

> Y : from their honeymoon—a ship on it named Princess—

> X : yes, and it's kind of funny, because he crashed onto her like a wave,
> and the ship broke open—

Q : Were there passengers?
> Y : Welts like rafts overlooked by a coast guard. But when she

moved in, we cut the shirt to dishrags.

Z : I got a robot.

Hunch once more over the display case.
Is there one in particular you'd like to see—

> The Fourth he met as X's horse-trainer.
> (This after the Second he again sequestered. After his breakdown—
> brain a cul-de-sac—*from French, "bottom of sack"*—thoughts couldn't
> pass through. Crazy, as in "bottom of your barrel.")

Colloquialism: Like Father, Like Son.
Exchange Son for Daughter,
Daughter for Y—she, too, collects:

> Lipsticks:
> The Second's: *mussels-clung-to-conch*
> The Third's: *orange-juice-sticky-in-the-fridge*
> And X's —because she's old enough now—*imprint-of-shoe-on-thigh*

> But this, *livers-on-a-cutting-board*, she's never seen, so
> questions the father,
> then answers the mother by putting the lipstick on her pillow (mole,
> definition 1.2: someone within a [family] who anonymously betrays
> confidential information).

Her mother read
the message
as if it were delivered
by the war department
to the front door
with a folded flag—

man

woman   woman

                    (a guardrail slammed into.
        Fur stuck in the car-grille—where's the animal?)

He was a blizzard that holed the Fourth
in his house. A degree that holds an ice sculpture to its form
heat ransacks.
After plastic surgery,
her urge to leave
made done.

A refresher course:

>   If he returns to the Second, like a Florida time-share visited a few weeks
>   each year, does it mean he likes the ocean? One rarely likes what's like him.
>
>   grain + grain + grain = beach
>   wife + wife + wife = husband
>
>   The issue is commonality. How one becomes many.
>   Example: a change purse and mouth are the same? Because they open.
>
>   If he is a mole (definition 1.3), hunger drives him out of his burrow.
>   The fertile feeding ground's revisited like a table covered with leftovers
>   for an effortless next meal.
>
>   Does this make the Second a dinner roll when he asks
>   *can somebody pass me some love?*

The first letter in his alphabet's *I do*. But he can't recall
the letters that follow.
So repeats it, hoping some brain-knob

will click and the rest will spill
like a knocked-over glass.

Fingerprints crud the display case.
Circle your sleeve against it:

> The Fifth: hair long as a tax-form.
> The Sixth: quick like a childhood hobby—a piano in the basement,
> and unskilled fingers that make it monotonous—Pop Goes the Weasel,
> Pop Goes the Weasel. Variations of speed. The Seventh:
> meek as a quarter-note.

Our subject just opened his office door.
Slide inquiries over the counter—remember how much better
a school chair moves with its feet in tennis balls—put a $20 under there.

Husband: Look at you lined up like bachelors—shouldn't I be asking the questions?

Question #1: What's the appeal?

H: What is the win that stops the gambler from quitting? Yes, we could make
this Jeopardy. My answers will be curtains hung on a rod of not-knowing.

> Question #2: Do you get them the same wedding bands?

H: Ah, but my favorite is Match Game—are you familiar with that one—the
host reads an unfinished pun, in hopes the celebrity panel will choose the same
word as the contestant. An example would be "Johnny the Butcher is a polyga-
mist; he gets for Christmas a new _____ set." Wife is the best answer. Wife
like Knife. Apropos, no?

> You're avoiding the questions.

H: The answers.

Your jaw's flashing like floor numbers in an elevator.

H: Going up or down?

If marriage is a structure, then what we have here is
a high-rise—which floor do you prefer?

H: For comfort? or finances, which, forgive me, I must return to—does a
refund seem fair?

Fairness, yes, let's get to fairness.

H: Have it your way. Leave them by the counter with an address.

scrap for grappling

1) Should I forgive him? Why, or why not?
a) *yes, my husband loves me*
b) *yes, he promised not to do it again*
c) *no, he hasn't asked to be forgiven*
d) *no, he doesn't deserve to be forgiven*

1-a) A sentence marries its verb—my sentence is an agreement to action.
1-b) A word is itself, so *again*, by its nature, is *again*—couldn't it also read *he promised again not to do it?*
1-c) I do not ask for morning, but expect it enough to set an alarm that I might enter it like a party I've been invited to.
1-d) A curious word, deserve. I know well the prefix *de-*. Opposite, or reverse. Deserve, the opposite of *serve*, which I vowed to do. Which he vowed. In the phrase "doesn't deserve," wouldn't the negative *n't* and *de-* cancel each other out—*he does serve to be forgiven.*

2) How do I come to terms?
a) *everything happens for a reason*
b) *happen reasons with self for everything*
c) *in the beginning, there was wait, which beget hope*
d) *self* is served through serving *Not-Self*

2-a) This sly trick—that non-committal *a.*
2-b) If I knew more jokes.
2-c) Wait is *hope's* offspring. Hope is the unmade bed and my body reclined in it. Hope is the balloon being filled with air, and wait the puncture.
2-d) It's the difference between *to heal* and *to be healed*—one must trust the Divine Editor and throw out her own red pen—how much nicer to eat out

than to prepare a meal, food arriving because you ordered it. Dressing on the side, extra cheese. Faith slaving in the kitchen, its goal to serve you. No human element to mess it up—a timer set incorrectly, the center a little too pink.

≈

Seasoned

There are certain cities frame-laid as winter—or me-winters I build
with numb thought. This time of separate pockets.
As separate pockets. Our distance is more
than glove-dense, meaning my hand—further than fabric from—

Fault all air conditioners that trek me back
to fog that obscures the castle—which backdrop I drop back to
because I remember best a nose in bridge light and snow
like a Xerox of snow. Here, a negative of our patented cold:
a zipper with broken teeth.

\+

How can you kiss me like paint when I ask
        that you kiss me like paint

                without my saying   over wood
                        over canvas/skin/the bin where murals are laid
                        like a bale in a barn, a veil during
                        the trying on rather than pride of

                        the dress

Also Available from saturnalia books:

Tsim Tsum by Sabrina Orah Mark

Days of Unwilling by Cal Bedient

To the Bone by Sebastian Agudelo
Winner of the Saturnalia Books Poetry Prize 2008

Letters To Poets: Conversations about Poetics, Politics, and Community
edited by Jennifer Firestone and Dana Teen Lomax

Famous Last Words by Catherine Pierce
Winner of the Saturnalia Books Poetry Prize 2007

Dummy Fire by Sarah Vap
Winner of the Saturnalia Books Poetry Prize 2006

Correspondence by Kathleen Graber
Winner of the Saturnalia Books Poetry Prize 2005

The Babies by Sabrina Orah Mark
Winner of the Saturnalia Books Poetry Prize 2004

Polytheogamy by Timothy Liu / Artwork by Greg Drasler
Artist/Poet Collaboration Series Number Five

Midnights by Jane Miller / Artwork by Beverly Pepper
Artist/Poet Collaboration Series Number Four

Stigmata Errata Etcetera by Bill Knott / Artwork by Star Black
Artist/Poet Collaboration Series Number Three

Ing Grish by John Yau / Artwork by Thomas Nozkowski
Artist/Poet Collaboration Series Number Two

Blackboards by Tomaz Salamun / Artwork by Metka Krasovec
Artist/Poet Collaboration Series Number One

Hush Sessions was printed using the fonts Avant Garde and Baskerville Crylic.

www.saturnaliabooks.com